klee

klee

Text by
MARCEL MARNAT

LEON AMIEL PUBLISHER
NEW YORK

Published by
LEON AMIEL PUBLISHER
NEW YORK, 1974
ISBN Number 8148-0589-2
© 1974 SPADEM
Printed in Italy

There are some revolutions that take place smoothly: it is almost as if the world were waiting for them. This was precisely the case with the plastic arts in 1910. The term plastic art can help us to define the sudden mutation that occurred then. Art had become serious business and it was believed that the "artist" could penetrate the unknown aspects of things, even if the effect produced was ultimately one of laughter. Romanticism, of course, had given

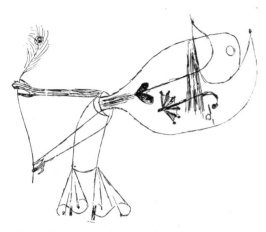

the artist a mission, making him responsible not only for illuminating the future but for providing indispensable revelations concerning the past. His job was similar to the scientist's in that he had to translate in a concise and durable language the multiple meanings of the universe, meanings that until then had remained too enigmatic to be perceived. The painter and sculptor made it easier to see nature (through the impact of their works) and, because they seemed to be visionaries, they accelerated history. Wilde wrote, "Nature imitates art," and art wished to exist in a more permanent form. Indeed, any indecisive or ambiguous qualities were banished from it, and the end of the nineteenth century confirmed the Goethean principle that poetry = truth.

Yet even before 1900 the idea of there being a unique plastic truth was attacked from all

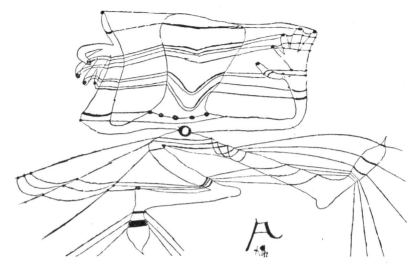

sides, as was the idea that nature could be reduced to a collection of formulas. The very reality of man himself as well as the stability of the universe were put into question. Einstein and Freud appeared, and the discovery of African, Polynesian and folk arts undermined the supremacy of the established arts and lowered the attendance figures for the *Mona Lisa.* All this gave rise to tremendous battles at the beginning of the century between the new forms of art that were just being born and a bourgeoisie not especially eager to see its visual habits disturbed, if not overthrown. It seemed as if Gauguin and the Fauves followed by the Cubists were destroying traditional pictorial comfort.

Today, with the perspective we have acquired,

it is easy to realize that these pioneers were doing no more than pursuing the logical development of art history. They carried the requirements of form, drawing, color and materials to a new level that had never been attained before. Their constant concern was to express more with a minimum of means. For a long time it has been explained that the pictorial revolution grew out of the systematic destruction of the practice of perspective. However, what was really responsible for liberating art from its institutional framework, its venerable heaviness, troubling monumentality and "humanistic" pretensions arose out of totally different premises. Nor did it take place in the bohemian and journalistic atmosphere of Montmatre. We must look toward Germany.

In effect, the big breakthrough occurred in 1910 in Munich when Kandinsky succeeded in composing a watercolor that intentionally did not represent anything. If we think about it, we can still feel the sense of dizzying excitement that must have been associated with this discovery, for a method of pictorial expression that could not be defined a priori as being "artistic" implied a new universe that no one yet knew anything about.

In 1910 Paul Klee was an enormously gifted young painter who was still looking for the precise form in which his genius would express itself. A superb draftsman, he was already admired for the disturbing figures he drew that had something of Blake, Goya and Beardsley about them... He was born in 1879 and, after

spending his childhood in Berne, had taken courses at the Academy of Fine Arts in Munich, a city that at that time was alive with painters and where all the new and exciting things that were happening in Paris were known and talked about in detail. Careful not to fall into any of the traps that were set by painting at the start of the century, Klee was particularly attracted by the traditional technique of glass painting. Klee was a Fauve at the same time as the Fauves were dazzling viewers with their riots of color, yet it is important to understand that whatever Klee did, he always did in a style that was uniquely his own. A picture dated 1905, *Garden Scene with Watering - Can (ill. 6),* would have displeased neither Vuillard (for the composition) nor Bonnard (for the color). The point of this is that from the start Klee was exceptionally open to the ideas that

were in the air; exceptionally cultivated as well. All of Klee's art consisted precisely in turning this mobility of spirit into the creative quality *par excellence*.

Between 1900 and 1940 Klee produced 9,146 works, a number that at first glance may seem suspicious and even unpardonable. What is truly miraculous is that these works contain an almost equal number of surprises. No other painter whose development took place along traditional lines could have produced so much without annoying repetitions. But, unlike one other notable example that could be mentioned, Klee's prolific output shows neither excesses nor complacencies, and the reason for this is simply that in his eyes the creative act consists in distilling the unexpected and the marvelous out of the dead matter of realism and in purifying them of all accidents and imperfections. He was concerned not with saying more but with saying less, provided of course that was said was of extreme ·rarity.

Klee's emergence as a painter coincided with a decisive and vulnerable moment in the history of art. The lessons of the so-called primitive arts were just being felt, and Kandinsky was opening the way to non-figurative expression. The success of the Cubists was combined with the explosive manifestations of the Futurists and Expressionists, all of whom accentuated this vulnerability by imparting an unexpected dynamism to objects, figures, and landscapes. In 1910 Klee gave up glass painting and "casually" articulated the surfaces of the *Girl with Jugs (ill. 3)*. To consider this work as Cubist would be to fail to take into account the attention that the painter paid to Robert Delaunay, who, that same year, exhibited his dynamic "Tour Eiffel." What fascinated Klee was less this dynamism than the way in which Cubism had transcended itself by restoring to the motif its essential *lightness*. Although it is relatively realistic, his *Girl with Jugs,* owing to the indecisive structure of its planes, does not seem to weigh anything. This step forward was actually as crucial and important as Kandinsky's non-figuration.

Paul Klee was a musician. As an adolescent, he had been torn between two vocations. Music, as an expression of an intangible world, certainly had all that was necessary to satisfy him. The composers who attracted him the most (Bach, Haydn, Mozart, Stravinsky) were precisely those

whose "cleanness" of style he admired. Indeed they foreshadow his pictorial concern always to leave the work clear and open and never to limit its message by including elements in it that might distract or scatter the viewer's attention. The Futurists celebrated the virtues of sound, speed and movement; Klee, on the other hand, was instinctively opposed to the general tumult which he resisted in an extraordinary way. He likewise escaped from "abstraction" even though he remained on friendly terms with Kandinsky until the end of his life. There is nothing in Klee's work that is directly suggestive of any of the great creative currents of this century; nor is there any intention to be "primitive." Klee described himself as being "somewhat closer to the hear of creation than usual," and the truth is that Klee represents

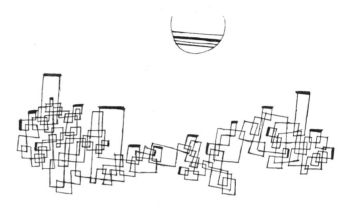

the spirit of creation before it is fixed or petrified in the mold of a given style.

Klee's ability to perceive the most infinitesimal vibrations at the heart of things explains the apparently effortless quality of his work and his formidable output. The voices that we can hear in his paintings are unexpected and at the same time familiar; part of the constant renewal of his vision, they also remind us of the forgotten voices of our own childhood dreams, fantasies and sometimes nightmares.

At a time when other art forms were enthusiastically absorbing the rhythms of modern life, of the city, train, airplane and subway, Klee's work distinguished itself by its silence. He listened eagerly to Kandinsky's descriptions of the bare landscapes of North Africa, the subtle relationships established between the lines of the desert horizon and the domes of Kairouan, between the huts of Hammamet and the blue of a Mediterranean that was neither Greek nor Roman. In spite of his education, Klee at all levels was already careful to eschew any humanist reference. In April, 1914, Klee visited Tunisia, and the twelve days he spent there confirmed beyond all expectation his need for silence and luminosity, his almost religious feeling for vast spaces. Significantly, Klee returned without delay to Germany, as if the sight of so many new images had dazzled him and he had to concentrate on translating them, not directly as did his companions Macke and Moilliet, but with all the means available to him in his studio. In spite of the outbreak of war on August 1, the year of 1914 was an exceptionally fruitful one for him. Mobilized, Klee served first in the infantry and then in an Air Force Reserve Unit. It seems he enjoyed some special privileges as he never was ordered to the front, and his main activity consisted in painting or varnishing airplanes. From the compact landscape of *In the Quarry* (1913, *ill. 2*) to the airy spaces of *Little Port* (1914, *ill. 1*), one can see that the luminosity of *Motif from Hammamet (ill. 4)* has intervened and that the painter had discovered one of his fundamental aesthetic orientations

The period immediately following the war was marked by an unprecedented intellectual confusion. In 1917 Dada broke out in Zurich with its corrosive nihilism and urge to destroy the ruling moral and social values. Klee's works

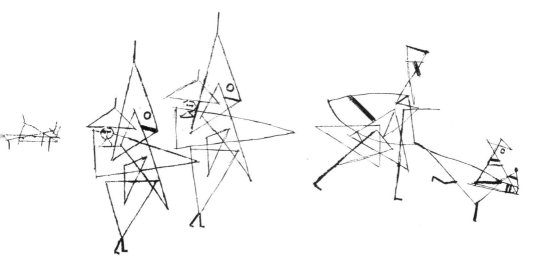

were included in the first exhibition of the group since they represented the negation of all previous aesthetic systems. In 1919 the architect Walter Gropius founded the Bauhaus in Weimar, a movement that brought together a group of German artists, architects and craftsmen who, using modern industrial materials, sought to provide a practical application of the arts in the modern world. In 1921 Klee was appointed a professor at the Bauhaus, and he taught glass painting and weaving at Weimar and Dessau until 1931. The "Surrealist Manifesto," published in Paris in 1924, did not fail to arouse his enthusiasm, and in October, 1929, René Crevel wrote the first French article devoted to Klee.

The paradox is that this painter who systematically made a point of remaining on the "outside" was attracted by all the new artistic movements, and that the name of this poet of silence was invoked by the most outspoken manifestations. But it can be safely said that there was absolutely no relationship between the character of the painter or of his works and the "1925" atmosphere or the extravagantly geometrizing tendencies of the "Art Deco" style. His aesthetic position was essentially solitary and would bring to mind that of the Italian "metaphysical painters" if it did not differ from it by the variety of themes that Klee methodically explored.

One of the most constant of these themes was undoubtedly his fondness for the landscape. Even when he was working on a plate of glass, using a technique that had been little developed, Klee had already captured the unusual aspects of nature. The confrontation between his own thought and its materialization in a landscape provided him with a means of verifying the accuracy of his researches. This can be seen, for example, in the transition between *Composition with a Black Center* (1919, *ill. 11*) and the sense of relief and space rediscovered in *Dream Landscape with Conifers* (1920, *ill. 12*). Similarly, the axonometric quality of *Arabian City* (1922, *ill. 10*) anticipates the more realistic vision of *Camp Road (ill. 17)* or *Settlement with Barracks (ill. 50)* ten years later. The tendency toward creating a light, airy structure can also be reversed, with the result that the viewer is then

plunged into a vision that is almost claustro-
phobic (as in *Picture of a Park, ill. 62; Young
Tree, ill. 57*). The horizon can even rise above
the upper edge of the picture (as in *Settlement
with Barracks, Highways and Byways, ill. 41*). Klee
is then led to "enclose" what ought to be free,
an irony that gives us the urban landscape
entitled *Hall of Singers (ill. 45)*, perhaps in order
to make us forget the memory of *Old Town and
Bridge (ill. 51)* which was painted two years
earlier.

The theme of the landscape is frequently
accompanied by a fairylike bestiary in which
irony and the fantasy of nursery rhymes exist
in a state of tension. Thus the drawing entitled
Heron (ill. 22) becomes the angry phantom of
The Bird Called Pep (ill. 23). The strident color
of *The Red Fish (ill. 36)* emits a scattering effect
as of light reflected in a mirror. This said, the
main subject is the one fish in the nocturnal
background that is not red... Klee's zoology
arises out of a dream world, and it encourages
him to depict humanity with as much distance
as humor.

A drawing like *Policeman Put to Flight* (1913)
or the self-portrait entitled *First Drawing for
the Phantom of a Genius* (1922) sets the tone for
Paul Klee's descriptions of human figures.
Contrary to his open-air visions, they represent
the other pole of his fantasy and are seen invariably in confined volumes, in theaters, for
instance, opera-houses or circuses. There are
the grotesque elements of *Fragment from a Ballet
for Aeolian Harp (ill. 13),* the sublimated graffiti

of *Puppet Theater (ill. 15)*, the dizzying sensation that we get from the brilliant graphism that supports the most distracted of tightrope walkers *(The Tightrope, ill. 20)*. *A Crusader (ill. 24)* seems to rise up out of the backstage of a derisory theater, and in *Clown (ill. 37)* which was also painted in 1929, Klee conveys an impression of solitude and tragic silence. Inevitably the painter interrogated masks, and it is in this perspective that we should read the rare paintings by his hand that evoke the primitive arts, such as *Barbarian Captain* (1932, *ill. 49*) or *From a Collection of Masks* (1938, *ill. 73*).

The third constant theme of his work constitutes in a way the antithesis of so many "spectacles": the study of the human figure or, to borrow Klee's more precise terminology, the study of "physiognomies." In fact, the human profile is rarely treated for its own sake in Klee's work or else it is seen in a deliberately humoristic perspective, as in *Naked on the Bed* (1939, *ill. 83*) or in a drawing of the same year entitled *Dialogue between a Man and a Tree* in which the knot of legs is suggestive of Picasso's most whimsical works. On the contrary, Klee is always serious when he depicts a face, whether it is a child's *(Child on the Steps, 1923, ill. 14; Senecio,* 1922, *ill. 16)* or images of adults who always seem strangely introspective: *Head with Blue Tones (ill. 54), Figure in the Garden (ill. 77)* and especially the famous *Scholar* of 1933 *(ill. 59)*. Gradually the viewer realizes that what counts in this art is not so much the emphasis given to a certain detail as the homogeneity

of the surface. This stands out clearly in the landscapes and is perceptible even in figurative descriptions such as *The Man of the Future* (1933, *ill. 60*).

Here we can see a final constant of Klee's art, his fondness for signs. Starting at the end of the war, they introduced a separate chapter into his work that opens with *Little Vignette for Egypt* (1918, *ill. 8*) and is continued by numerous examples of imaginary writing *(Document, 1933, ill. 65)*. A whole universe of symbols thus grew up in the midst of a pictorial equilibrium that was unfailingly maintained. The most extremes examples of this are *17 IRR* (1923, *ill. 28*) and the figurative symbols scattered in *Full*

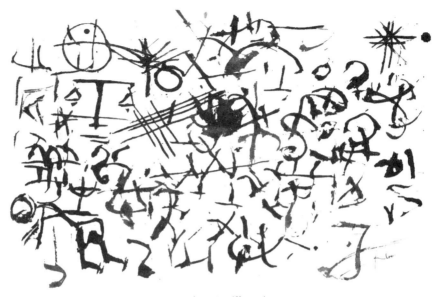

Moon (1927, *ill. 29*).

This exploration led Klee to the verge of abstraction, as is evident in the transition from *Little Picture of Dice* (1925, *ill. 30*) to *Cloisonné* (1928, *ill. 31*) or to *Mixed Weather* (1929, *ill. 33*). It seems as if Klee actually entered abstraction with the graphic enigmas of *Composition (ill. 38)* or of *Six Types* (1930, *ill. 42*) but at once he checked himself and gave his least figurative creations titles that seem to anchor them in reality: *Sailing City (ill. 43), Hovering (about to Take off, ill. 44), Model of a Flower Vase (ill. 46), Free but Securely Held (ill. 47), Open (ill. 55),* etc. At the same time he came back to the use of sign-symbols, as can be seen in *Gate of the*

*Deserted Garden (ill. 76), Serpentines (ill. 58),
Pond with Swans (ill. 64), With the Two Lost Ones
(ill. 81).* From then on even the simplified
representation of the human figure could force-
fully reassert itself, as in *Oh! But oh! (ill. 67),
The Way out at Last (ill. 69), Pomona (ill. 72),*
or, in the last year of his life, the ironic *Egyptian
Woman (ill. 87)* as well as the hieratic condensa-
tion of a *Drummer* (1940, *ill. 86*).

So much irony and reserve, so many distances
taken with respect to a century that was particularly proud of its conquests, did not go
without some anguish, and it would be a mistake
to see in Klee no more than the unexpected
painter of an ever-renewed spirit of invention
and freshness. The disturbing figures that he
created at the beginning of his career reappeared
periodically like the signs of a quickly concealed
anguish. The menacing atmosphere of the
Materialized Ghosts (1923, *ill. 18*) cannot be seen
simply as picturesque, nor can the nightmarish
effect of *Fear behind the Curtain* (1929, *ill. 40*)
be forgotten so easily. In 1935 Paul Klee began
to suffer from the multiple sclerosis that five
years later was to prove fatal. Despite the seren-
ity with which the artist seems to have borne
his illness, the work of his last period was
progressively overshadowed by it as well as by
the more and more precise threats of war that
on account of Nazism were hanging over Europe.
Klee came back to Berne in 1933 and did not
leave Switzerland again. In 1937 the Nazis
confiscated one hundred and seven of his works;
seventeen of them were shown at the exhibition

of "Degenerate Art" that was organized in Munich. Braque and Picasso then visited him in Switzerland and Klee continued to work without interruption. But the increasing fantasy of his inspiration was often contradicted by the harshness of his titles (for instance, *Severe Countenance* of 1939). Many of his drawings also alluded to the political agitation: *Fraternity* (1939). From the same year, it is true, dates the lively series of *Angels,* another example of the way Klee always managed to coordinate extremes. The illustrations of this book end with one of the most striking images of death in all of twentieth century art, the tiny picture entitled *Death and Fire (ill. 88)*—a pitiless grimace in an apocalyptic environment. Paul Klee died near Locarno on June 29, 1940, shortly before World War II was declared.

The way Klee resisted aesthetic currents and fashions was all the more remarkable in that his reputation as an artist and teacher quickly spread throughout the world (he exhibited in New York in 1924). The creative revolution that Klee brought about arose quietly out of an almost philosophical context, and this is why other avant-garde artists found his example so fascinating. Klee summed up his own attitude in a key phrase: "Art does not reproduce what can be seen: it makes things visible."

We have spoken about Klee's themes and tried to explain his point of departure. But Klee also had to find a plastic translation that would be suitable to the expression of his ideas and his peculiar genius. Here also Klee did not fall into the trap of being overly demonstrative. The very size of his pictures and drawings indicates his awareness of this and his care to avoid sweeping affirmations. Klee actually never worked on a large scale, refusing the "luxury" of those large pictures saturated with forms and colors that Parisian painters refer to familiarly as "pies." The format of a drawing notebook or of a small-scale frame was enough for him. In this way he produced an endless number of drawings: scumbles, scrapings, works done with chalk, with paste... But his pictorial substance was never rich, he never used varnishes, skillfully translucent colors, or impastoes. On the contrary, his substance was plastery, opaque, as if avariciously rubbed on the support which indeed often reappeared between the painted surfaces. The colors he used, however, were luminous, and his excessively dried oils look as if their only concern were to mimic the refinements of the watercolor. Klee, besides, was particularly fond of the technique of watercolor, as can be seen by the number of his watercolors which is five times greater than that of his oil paintings. Only his drawings are more numerous (nearly five thousand).

Once the keyboard had been defined, it remained to play upon it. It seems that for Paul Klee the creative act was extremely private; even those closest to him never saw the way in which he moved from concept to execution, from the poetic to the pictorial. It is known, however, that contrary to the practices of most other painters, especially in recent times, Klee

always had several works in the fire at the same time, usually involving different techniques. Undoubtedly the agility that allowed him to jump from one subject to another helped him to avoid any heaviness, as the balance established in one work made him better able to perceive any fat that had grown on another. Most significantly, it seems that Klee started to create without having a precise idea about what the final result would be. He moved like a medium between different sketches and preliminary studies, distributing here and there the ideas and suggestions that grew out of the silence at the center of his creative being. His pictures, born out of chance encounters with matter, thus may be compared with those fractional crystallizations that can be obtained from a complex solution. Klee himself pretended to be astonished by the individuality of some of the results he achieved. From then on the work was considered to be finished and was put away in a corner.

A second extremely important stage in his creative process then occurred. It consisted precisely in his giving titles to the works he has recently finished working on. The forms and substance had now blossomed, and a whole series of fleeting visions had left their imprint on the picture. Klee had to proceed to what he jokingly referred to as a "baptismal ceremony." An extensive study could be made of Paul Klee's titles, not only for their charm or poetic quality but above all for the relationships they establish with the picture itself, to which they add another dimension, or which they contradict, with an ever renewed sense of humor. It is enough to think of those birds chirping away on an elegantly stretched wire—the wire extended by the most incongruous of cranks—and the result becomes the famed *The Twittering Machine (ill. 19)* which is guaranteed to make every musician dream.

Klee proceeded in the same way throughout his life. The extraordinary aesthetic unity that underlies his work makes it possible to see each period as an unbroken part of a whole.

Undoubtedly it would have been very difficult to date his works if Klee himself had not kept a meticulous record of them.

The extreme seriousness that was hidden beneath a charming sense of humor, his quickness in retaining the most essential aspects of so many ephemeral visions, his extraordinary and above all immediate success with so many different audiences, even the most unprepared— everything, in short, seems to point to Klee's being a facile painter. Yet there is something shocking about the very use of this term with respect to Klee. If we want to find the reasons for this new contradiction, we must look elsewhere. Klee's moral and aesthetic engagement

was in fact total and, in the last analysis, the very scope of his accomplishments will help us to understand the mutation that took place as of 1910.

The reason we cannot think of Klee as a "facile" painter is that the charm that is so generally felt with regard to his work was born less from a series of recipes (even if they were new) than from a series of refusals. What Klee refused was to work within the limits of a single technique or manner. He refused likewise to listen to anyone, even the most glorious (the Cubist, the Expressionists); he refused both traditional figuration as well as non-figuration; finally he refused the habitual prestige of a highly worked pictorial surface (with conglomerations of "matter," masterly colors, drawing for drawing's sake...) This string of refusals should have led him to sterility, to nothingness, to a desperate sense of humor, to the famous "white square on a white background" that Malevich proposed in Russia.

But Klee never knew such desperation because he was the first (and perhaps the only one) to have realized that the heights of pure abstraction, whatever their grandeurs (Mondrian) or their seductions (Kandinsky), were never anything more than an ultimate and logical consequence of the general movement of art history. The series of drawings that shows how Mondrian passed from a tree à la Van Gogh to a "cold" geometrical composition based on intersecting vertical and horizontal lines is familiar to everyone today. But Klee (who may or may not have been aware of such predictable decantations) managed to maintain his independence through his discovery that even this "abstract" art was not free of the traditional demonstrative vocation. That is to say, even Mondrian demonstrates something, even Kandinsky teaches one how to see, and Picasso or Braque even more so. Similarly, even the "anti-painting" of a Miró, for example, was fatally destined to be assimilated by, and made part of, the evolution of art history. The only ones who escaped from this assimilation where the Italian "metaphysical" painters who, from early Chirico to Morandi, reversed the tendency by painting enigmas. Klee undoubtedly was acquainted with their works early in his career, but his genius was to manifest similar preoccupations that were free of any weight and thus were expressed in less realistic terms. In this way, in its invariably recognizable variety, Klee's painting remains outside of time. Like the sphinx that it was at the time of the First World War, it has kept all its power of surprise—an uncomfortable surprise, an emotional impact. Each time we see it Klee's painting acts deep within us at an unforeseeable level of our consciousness.

Klee was the first painter who did not depict on the canvas the solutions he had found to previous aesthetic problems. He does not offer any answers to questions that the viewer is not obliged to ask. On the contrary, Klee's work represents the question itself. This is why he preoccupied all the avant-garde movements. Everyone can identify with his painting to the degree that his light hues and unconstrained forms seem to correspond exactly to our thirst and endlessly postponed interrogations. Why is it that his pictures seem as familiar to us as if they were part of our deepest selves? They express our curiosity in its keenest and rarest form—the most dulled also by our "civilization." Like the vision of Kairouan in the past, the pictures of Paul Klee wake us up, and soon we find that they have become an indispensable part of us because they substitute for all time the vital ardor of the questions which they incarnate for the fixity of final solutions.

Translated by
Wade Stevenson

BIOGRAPHY

1879
Birth at Münchenbucksee near Berne. His father, who is music master at the training school for teachers at Berne-Hofwyl, is German; his mother is Swiss.

1880
The Klee family—father and mother, Paul and his sister Mathilde—born in 1876—settles in Berne.

1886-1898
Klee attends primary school and the Berne Gymnasium. Takes his *Matura*. At the age of seven he learns to play the violin.

1898
Klee goes to Munich and enters Knirr's school of art. He once more meets the sculptor Hermann Haller, whom he had known since 1886.

1899
In the autumn meets the pianist Lily Stumpf (born 1876), daughter of a Munich doctor; she will become his wife in 1906.

1900
Attends the Munich Academy in Franz Stuck's studio where Kandinsky is also present.

1901-1902
Leaves the Academy and goes on a journey to Italy with Hermann Haller. Does not return to Berne until 1906.

1903-1905
Klee produces his first ten etchings. Plays a great deal of music and is violonist in the Berne municipal orchestra. First "sous-verres." Klee visits Paris along with his Swiss friends Hans Bloesch and Louis Moilliet. The Fauves exhibit in the Salon d'Automne.

1906
Klee exhibits six etchings at the Sezession in Munich. Marriage to Lily Stumpf. He settles in Munich. In order to support them his wife teaches music while he looks after the house.

1907
Klee submits etchings and "sous-verres" to Karl Scheffler who refuses to publish them in *Kunst und Künstler*. Three sous-verres—which he submits to the jury of the Munich Sezession are also rejected. Birth of his only child, Felix.

1908
The *Bund Zeichnender Künstler,* an association of artists interested in drawing, refuses to make him a member. The Debschitz

School employs him for some months to supervise its evening classes for drawing from the nude. The Munich Sezession, to which he sends six of his "sous-verres," accepts only three. He offers the etching *Hero with a Wing* to Franz Biel for the review *Hyperion*. Never published. Sends six drawings to the Berlin Sezession which exhibits them in its Black and White Salon.

1909

Klee describes an exhibition by Hans von Marées at the Munich Sezession as "an event." He sees eight pictures by Cézanne at the Sezession and discovers in him the master *par excellence* who teaches him much more than Van Gogh. The Berlin Sezession exhibits some of his work.

1910

Klee exhibits 56 of his works from the years 1907-1910 at the Berne Museum, at the Zurich Kunsthaus and in a gallery in Winterthur. One of his drawings is acquired by Alfred Kubin (born in 1877).

1911

The exhibition organized in Berne the year before is shown in Basel. The critic Wilhelm Michel submits some of Klee's drawings to the editor of the review *Kunst und Dekoration,* who refuses to publish them, and to the Munich art dealer, Thannhauser, who agrees to exhibit thirty of them in the corridor of his gallery. Klee is one of the founder-members of *Sema*—an association of artists which includes, among others, Kubin, Caspar and Scharff. He meets Kandinsky, Franz Marc, Campendonck, Mariane von Werefkin, Gabriela Münter and Arp.

1912

Klee participates in the second exhibition of the *Blaue Reiter* group, held in the Goltz Gallery and composed entirely of drawings and etchings. He visits Paris and meets Delaunay, Le Fauconnier, Picasso, Karl Wolfskehl, the friend of Stefan George.

1913

Klee exhibits in the Sturm Gallery and takes part in the same gallery in the first German Salon d'Automne which presents a wide survey of modern European art with 360 pictures.

1914

Klee is one of the founders of the New Munich Sezession—a group instigated by the critic Wilhelm Hausenstein; Marc and Kandinsky do not take part. Journey to Tunisia in the company of Moilliet and Macke. Ist August: outbreak of war. Marc, Macke and Campendonck are mobilized. Kandinsky, Jawlensky, Mariane von Werefkin and Gabriele Münter leave Germany. Klee stays on in Munich.

1915

Klee receives a visit from Rilke. Goes to Switzerland with the permission of the German military authorities. Begins modelling and coloring statuettes.

1916

Klee mobilized in the Landsturm.

1918

Remains at Gersthofen until after the armistice. Towards Christmas demobilized and returns to his family in Munich. In Berlin, Walden publishes the *Sturm Bilderbuch* made up of drawings from *Der Sturm,* including 15 drawings by Klee.

1919

In Munich Klee rents a

large studio in the Suresnes Palace. Two painters, Baumeister and Schlemmer, try to have him taken on as professor at the Stuttgart Academy, but he is turned down. He signs a contract with the art dealer Goltz. Kahnweiler begins to buy his pictures.

1920

Big exhibition in Munich at Goltz's gallery with 362 works. The Berlin review *Tribüne der Kunst und Zeit,* edited by Kasimir Edschmid publishes *Creative Confession* which Klee began to write in 1918. His illustrations for *Candide,* which date from 1911, are published by Kurt Wolff in Munich. Another work illustrated by Klee—Curt Corrinth's *Postdamer Platz*—is published by Georg Müller in Munich. Hans von Wedderkop and Leopold Zahn each devote a monograph to him. On 25th November Klee is invited to become a professor at the Bauhaus.

1921

He leaves Munich for Weimar. At the Bauhaus he teaches glass painting and weaving. Later also teaches oil painting. Wilhelm Hausenstein publishes his monograph *Kairouan,* or *The History of the Painter Klee and the Art of our Time.*

1922

Takes part in exhibitions at Wiesbaden and Berlin.

1923

He publishes *Ways of Studying Nature* in the publication *Staatliches Bauhaus in Weimar 1919-1923.* Exhibits in the Kronprinzenpalast in Berlin.

1924

First exhibition in the United States in New York. Foundation in Weimar of the *Blauen Vier* group: Kandinsky, Klee, Feininger and Jawlensky. Léon-Paul Fargue visits Klee in Weimar. Voyage to Sicily. Klee gives a lecture in Jena *On Modern Art;* it is not published until 1945. The Bauhaus is compelled to shut down in Weimar.

1925

Teachers and pupils of the Bauhaus settle in Dessau. Klee publishes his *Pedagogical Sketches* in the series Bauhaus-Bücher. Second large exhibition of 214 works in Goltz's gallery. Takes part in the first exhibition of Surrealist painters held in Paris at the Pierre Gallery along with Arp, De Chirico, Ernst, Miró, Picasso and others. First one-man exhibition in Paris at the Vavin-Raspail Gallery.

1926-1928

Klee goes to Italy, stays on Porquerolles and in Corsica, visits Brittany and Belle-Isle. The Kleegesellschaft founded by the collector Otto Rahlfs of Brunswick offers him a trip to Egypt. In the Bauhaus review he publishes *exact Experiment in the Realm of Art.*

1929

Journey to the South of France. For Klee's fiftieth birthday the Flechtheim Gallery in Berlin organizes a large exhibition of his works. Exhibition in the Bernheim Jeune Gallery in Paris. Will Grohmann publishes a monograph in the *Cahiers d'Art.*

1930

Klee spends some time in the Engadine and at Viareggio. Another exhibition in Flechtheim's Gallery. Exhibition in the Museum of Modern Art of New York. Member of the committee and jury of the *Deutscher Künstlerbund.*

1931

Klee terminates his contract

with the Bauhaus and accepts a chair offered to him by the Düsseldorf Academy. Finds Campendonck there. Among the other professors there is Matisse's former pupil, Oskar Moll, as well as the sculptors Alexander Zschokke and Ewald Mataré.

1932
Journey to Switzerland and Italy (Venice). Under pressure from the Nazis the Bauhaus leaves Dessau and settles in Berlin (Freies Bauhaus).

1933
Journey to the South of France: St.-Raphaël, Hyères, Port-Cros. Klee is violenty attacked by the Nazis and is finally dismissed. About Chritstmas time he leaves Germany and settles permanently in Switzerland. He once more installs himself in Berne where his father and sister are still living.

1934
First Klee exhibition in England at the Mayor Gallery in London. Kahnweiler becomes Klee's dealer. Grohman publishes a collection of his drawings in Germany; the book is confiscated by the Nazis.

1935
Large retrospective exhibition in the Kunsthalle, Berne. First symptom of the illness—sclerodermia—which will lead to his death five years later.

1936
His illness depresses him and he works little. He takes treatment at Tarasp and Montana without appreciable results.

1937
Klee resumes his work. Stay at Ancona where he visits the widow of Franz Marc. Ernst Ludwig Kirchner who lives near Davos comes to see him as do Picasso and Braque. Sees Kandinsky for the last time on the occasion of an exhibition of Kandinsky's work in the Kunsthalle, Berne. The Nazis include 17 works by Klee in the exhibition of "Degenerate Art," at first in Munich and later in other German cities. They confiscate 102 of them from public collections and auction them.

1938
Klee is represented at the Bauhaus exhibition organized by the Museum of Modern Art in New York. He exhibits in New York at the Buchholtz and Nierendorf Gallery and in Paris at Kahnweiler's and Carré's.

1939
Klee rests by a lake near Berne.

1940
Large Klee exhibition in the Kunsthaus, Berne, of works dated 1935-1940. On June 28 dies at Muralto-Locarno.

1942
In September the urn containing Klee's ashes is interred in the Schlosshalde cemetery in Berne.

LIST OF PLATES

PLANCHES

PLATES

1
Petit Port
1914
Little Port

2 Dans la carrière. 1913. In the Quarry.

3
Fillette aux cruches
1910
Girl with Jugs

4
Motif d'Hamammet
1914
Motif from Hamammet

6
Scène de jardin
avec arrosoirs
1905
Garden Scene
with Watering-Can

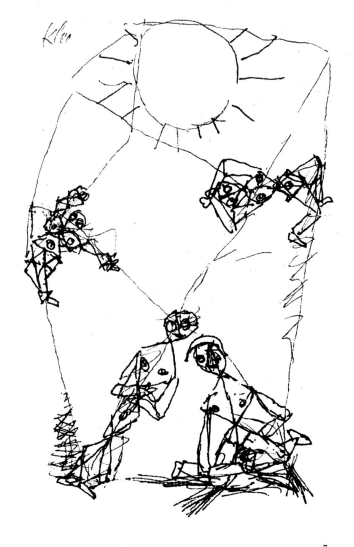

7
Faiblesse humaine
1913
Human Weakness

8
Petite Vignette
pour l'Égypte
1918
Little Vignette
for Egypt

9
Sous l'étoile noire
1918
Under a Black Star

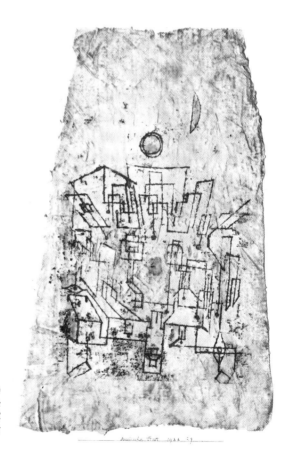

10
Ville arabe
1922
Arabian City

11 Composition au centre noir. 1919. Composition with a Black Center.

12 Paysage de rêve aux conifères. 1920. Dream Landscape with conifers.

13
Fragment d'un ballet
sur des airs de
harpe éolienne
1922 ?
Fragment from
a Ballet for
Aeolian Harp

14
Enfant sur le perron
1923
Child on the Steps

15
Théâtre de marionnettes
1923
Puppet Theatre

16
Senecio
1922

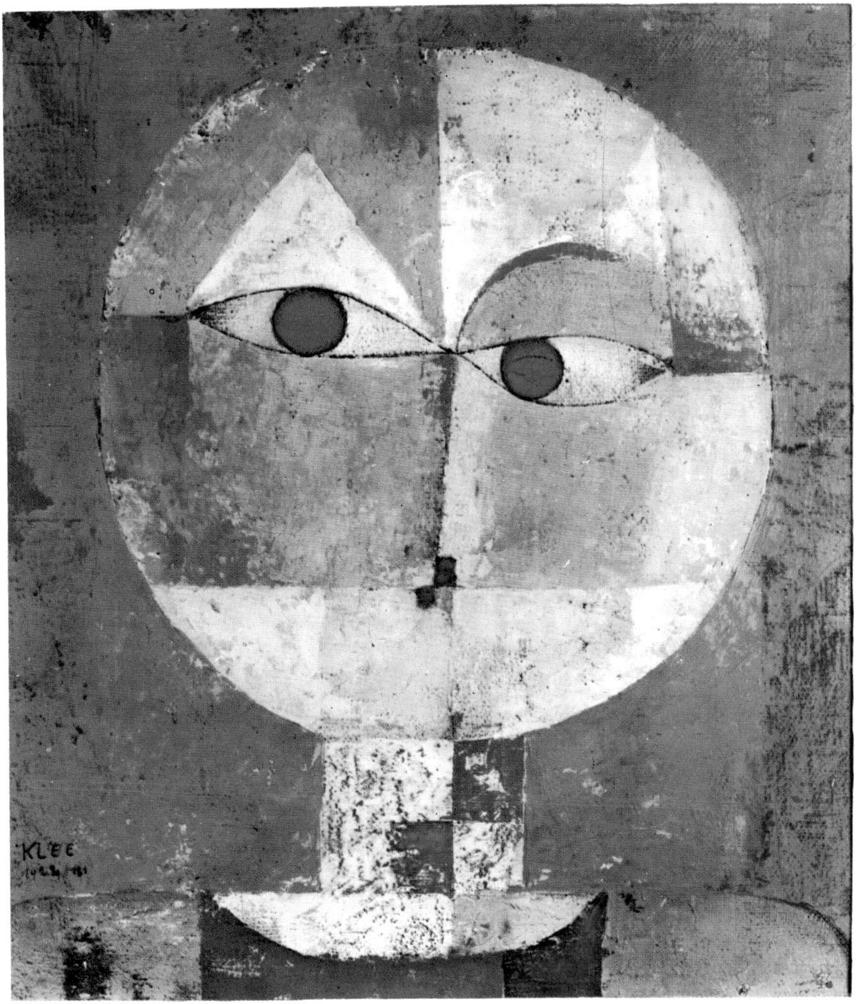

17 Route dans le camp. 1923. Camp Road.

19
La Machine à gazouiller
1922
The Twittering Machine

20
Le Funambule
1923
The Tightrope
Walker

21
Ab Ovo
1917

1977.130.

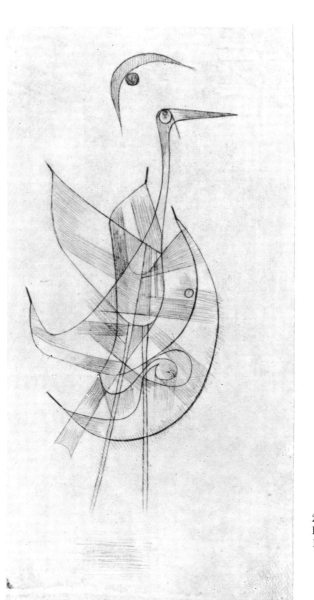

22
Héron
1924

23   L'Oiseau Pep. 1925. The Bird Called Pep.

24
Un Croisé
1929
A Crusader

25 Carnaval en montagne. 1924. Carnaval in the Mountains.

26
Ville pavoisée
1927
Flagged Town

27   Résonance de la flore méridionale. 1927. Resonance of the Southern Flora.

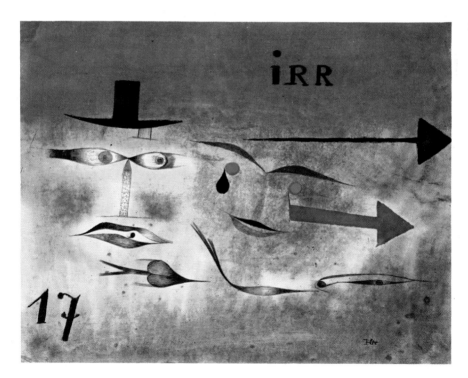

29 Pleine Lune. 1927. Full Moon.

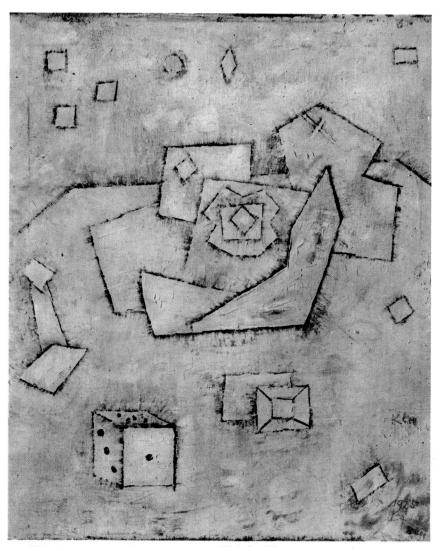

30
Petite Image
aux dés
1925
Little Picture
of Dice

31 Cloisonné. 1928.

32
Avant la neige
1929
Before the Snow

34 La Place des jumeaux. 1929. The Twin's Place.

35
Figuier
1929
Figtree

36
Le Poisson rouge
1925
The Red Fish

38 Composition 1930

39   Feuille en pleine lumière. 1929. Illuminated Leaf.

40 Angoisse derrière la fenêtre. 1929. Fear Behind the Curtain.

41
Chemin principal
et chemin latéraux
1929
Highway and Byways

42   Six Espèces. 1930. Six Types.

44
En suspens
(sur le point de s'élever)
1930
Hovering
(About to Take off)

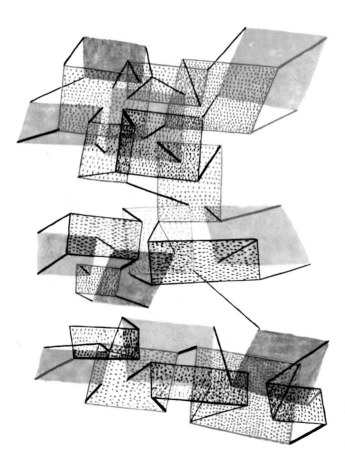

43
Ville flottante
1930
Sailing City

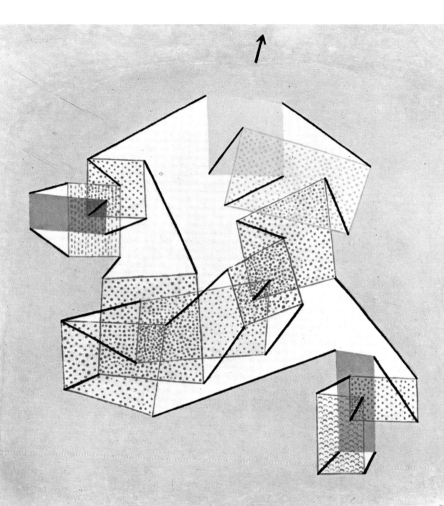

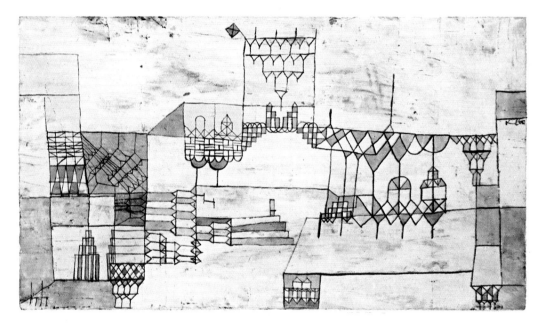

45 La Salle des chanteurs. 1930. Hall of Singers.

46
Modelé d'un
vase à fleurs
1930
Model of
a Flower Vase

47   Libre, mais rigoureusement contenu. 1930. Free but Securely Held.

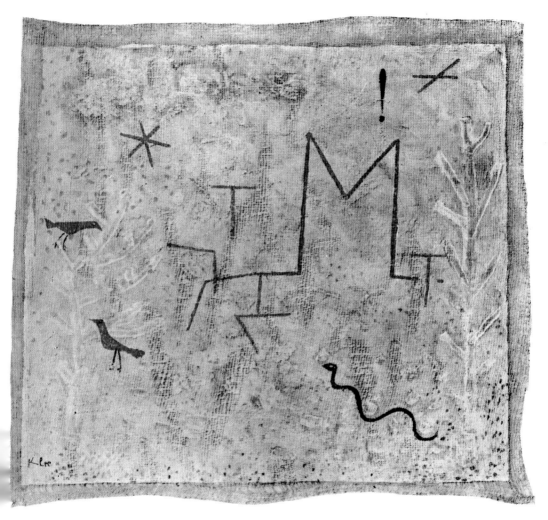

48 Porte de jardin M. 1932. Garden Gate M.

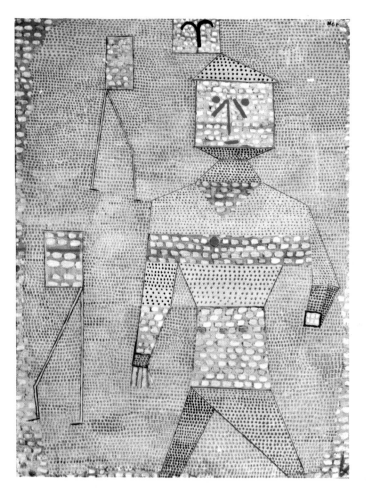

49
Capitaine barbare
1932
Barbarian Captain

51   Vieille Ville et Pont. 1928. Old Town and Bridge.

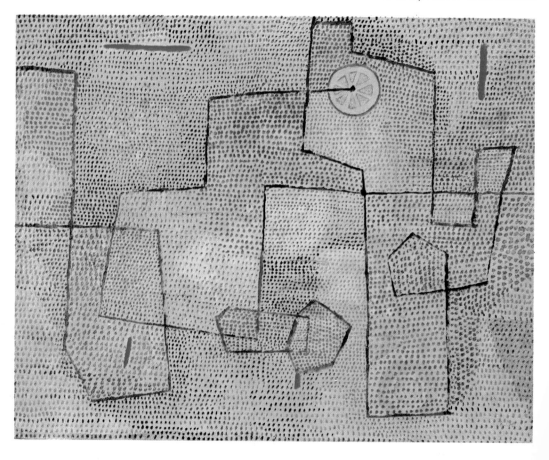

53
Gamme de couleurs
(dominante grise)
1930.
Table of colour
(in Grey Major)

54
Tête aux tons bleus
1933
Head with Blue Tones

55 Ouvert. 1933. Open.

56
Petit Diable bleu
1933
Little Blue Devil

57
Jeune Arbre
(Chloranthenum)
1932
Young Tree

59
Le Savant
1933
Scholar

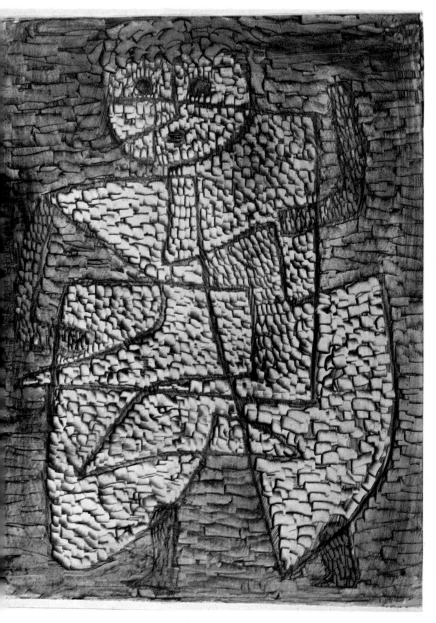

60
L'Homme de dema[...]
1933
The Future Man

51 Masque brisé. 1934. Broken Mask.

62
Parc
1933
Picture of
a Park

63 Diane dans le vent d'automne.
1934. Diana in the Autumn Wind.

64
L'Étang aux cygnes
1937
Pond with Swans

66
Arctique meublé
1935
Furnished Arctic

67
Hélas ! Oh hélas !
1937
Oh ! But oh !

8 Deux Fruits formant paysage. 193?. Two Fruit Landscape.

69   L'Issue enfin trouvée. 1935. The Way out at Last.

71   Jardin qui vient d'être aménagé. 1937. Newly Laid out Garden.

72
Pomone
1938

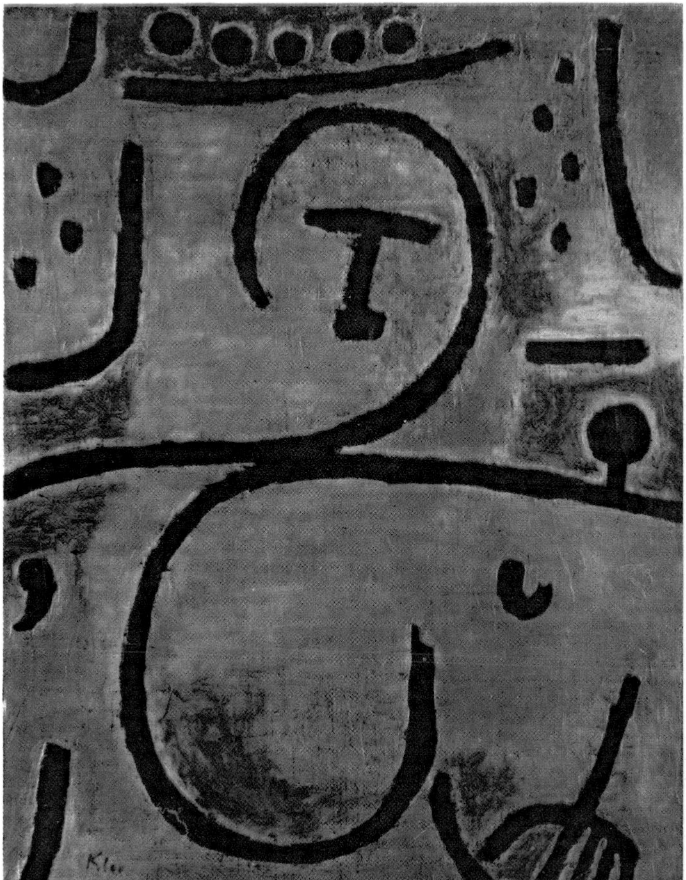

73
D'une collection de masques
1938
From a Collection of Maskes

74   Vert sur vert. 1938. Green on Green.

76   Porte du jardin délaissé. 1935. Gate of the Deserted Garden.

77
Figure au jardin
1937
Figure in the Garden

78
Arbre dans la ville
1939
Tree in the Town

79
La Coupe du serpent
1938
Severing of the Snake

80
Veut s'embarquer
1939
Wants to go Aboard

81
Avec les deux égarés
1938
With the Two Lost Ones

82
Le Parc d'Abien
1939
The Park at Abien

83 Nu sur le lit. 1939. Naked on the Bed.

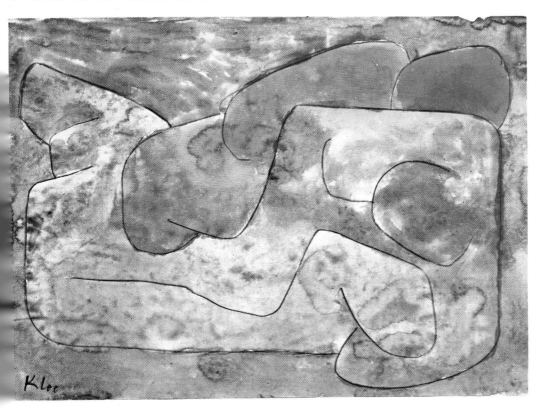

84
Avec des bas verts
1939
With Green Stockings

85
Pauvre Ange
1939
Poor Angel

86
Timbalier
1940
Drummer

87
Égyptienne
1940
Egyptian Woman

88   La Mort et le Feu. 1940. Death and Fire.